GEL CANDLES

To my mother
Doris Irene Constable
1911 - 2001

GEL CANDLES

David Constable

SEARCH PRESS

First published in Great Britain 2002

Search Press Limited
Wellwood, North Farm Road,
Tunbridge Wells, Kent TN2 3DR

Text copyright © David Constable
Photographs by Lotti de la Bédoyère, Search Press Studios
Photographs and design copyright © Search Press Ltd. 2002

ISBN 1 903975 12 13

The Publishers and author can accept no responsibility for any
consequences arising from the information, advice or instructions
given in this publication.

Readers are permitted to reproduce any of the candles in this
book for their personal use, or for the purposes of selling for
charity, free of charge and without the prior permission of the
Publishers. Any use of the candles for commercial purposes is not
permitted without the prior permission of the Publishers.

If you have difficulty obtaining any of the equipment or materials
mentioned in this book, please write to the author David
Constable at Candle Makers Supplies, 28 Blythe Road, London
W14, telephone 0044 (0)207 602 4031 or visit the website
candles@candlemakers.co.uk

I would like to thank my editor Alison Howard,
photographer Lotti de la Bédoyère, James Adams,
Clint Twist and others too numerous to mention
individually. Thanks also to my customers, who
continue to inspire me with their enthusiasm.

Publishers' note
All the step-by-step photographs in this book feature the
author, David Constable, demonstrating how to make gel
candles. No models have been used.

Printed in Spain by Elkar S. Coop. Bilbao 48012

Cover: **Bowl with three wicks**
*This candle was made very simply by fixing three wicks to the
bottom of a shallow glass container, colouring some gel with wax
dye, then filling up the bowl.*

Page 1: **Clock works**
*An old clock which had stopped was given a new lease of life by
taking it apart and embedding its workings in layers of gel.*

Page 2: **Shell candle**
*A wick and a few pretty shells were fixed to the bottom of a small,
straight-sided container which was filled with clear gel.*

Page 3: **Oyster shell**
*A large fish bowl is an ideal container for an embedded shell –
look closely and you might discover a pearl!*

Opposite: **Time candle**
*Brass curtain rings embedded at intervals in a tall, narrow
container measure the passing of time as the candle burns down.*

Contents

Introduction

It is a rare and precious time when the introduction of a new and modern material so transforms a traditional craft. In one sense, gel candles are just a variation on the container candles which have become increasingly popular in recent years. In another, much more real sense, gel candles represent a quantum leap for candle making.

To experience the size and potential of this leap, I invite you to light a gel candle in a darkened room and simply watch it glow. I defy anyone who possesses the slightest degree of creativity not to be truly inspired by the radiant possibilities of candle gel.

The simplest and slightest intervention – the merest hint of colour can be enough, or just a sprinkle of glitter – can transform a candle which is already beautiful into something quite outstanding. The pigments or dyes used to colour candles can be opaque, so they look like regular candles, or transparent, allowing natural light to shine through them during the day. Colour can also be swirled through the gel to create three-dimensional effects.

Within the container, the gel itself can become a receptacle for souvenirs and mementoes. This provides the additional fascination of working in miniature, creating tiny tableaux embedded in clear gel. Though these candles can, of course, be lit on special occasions, the candles are just as likely to be kept as a reminder of happy memories.

A large part of my excitement about candle gel is that it is a developing technology, with a stream of improvements and innovations in the pipeline. At the time of writing this introduction, gel candles have to be made with wicks that were really designed for use with paraffin wax candles. These paper- and zinc-cored wicks are adequate, but manufacturers could do better. A true bubble-free gel, which can be cast easily into layers, is another development which must be just around the corner. Freestanding gel, which can be used without a container, is sure to follow soon. One thing is sure: the full potential of gel candles is yet to be realised. I hope this book will provide the inspiration for you to be part of the exciting future of gel candles.

David Constable

Opposite:
Treasure chest

Gravel is an excellent base for scenes like this one, but trapped air can bubble up and spoil the look of your candle. To overcome this, put the gravel in a container, cover with gel, and put the container into a slow oven for a few hours to 'cook' out the trapped air. Remove and allow to cool before arranging the items you want to embed. Some attractive rocks and shells, a toy treasure chest and some junk jewellery make a candle which is a real treasure.

Materials

Gel for candles can be bought ready-coloured, but I generally use clear gel and add my own pigment or dye. This is very easy to do, and the bonus is that it gives you a colour palette limited only by your imagination and your ability to mix the shades you want.

When you buy gel, you may be offered different grades including 'low-melt' and 'bubble-free'. I tend to use the so-called 'bubble-free', but a word of warning: even this will form bubbles if you pour the molten gel too quickly. Slow and steady is the first rule of making gel candles. You may have to practise to achieve this, and the first ones you make may have quite a few bubbles, but this effect can be regarded as part of the charm of the candle.

If you do have a real disaster with a candle, try this simple trick. Put the container in a slow oven for a few minutes to 'cook', until air bubbles rise to the surface. You can even re-melt a set candle in this way, and cook it gently until the bubbles disappear. Note that this only works for one-colour candles with no embedded items.

wicks and sustainers

Candle wicks come in three gauges: fine, medium and thick. The size of candle usually dictates the choice of wick, but medium is a good all-round choice for beginners. Those with metal cores are stiffer and tend to be easier to work with. Wicks are often used with sustainers, small metal discs which are clamped round the wick using pliers and can be fixed to the container.

shellac

(1, above) If an item you wish to embed in a candle is porous, paint on shellac to seal it. Let it dry thoroughly before using it.

methylated spirit

(2) Use this to give your glass containers extra sparkle before making up your candles.

paraffin wax

(3) Melt these small white beads down and drop wicks in the wax to stiffen them.

silica gel

(4) These fine, white crystals absorb moisture, and can be used to dry flowers and foliage before embedding them in gel.

adhesive

(5) Use this to fix items to the bottom of containers.

Gel, wick sustainers and wicks in different grades

containers

You can make a gel candle in virtually any container, from an ordinary tumbler to a large fish tank. Glass is ideal because it makes the most of the effect of the glowing colours of the translucent gel. A look round any kitchen will reveal any number of suitable containers, from ordinary jam jars to vases and pretty glasses. You may also be inspired by junk-shop finds. The oil-based gel is easy to remove from the container at any time should you want to return it to its original use.

One of the main things to watch out for is that your chosen container must be able to withstand the heat of the molten gel; thermal shock can sometimes cause fine china or glass to shatter. If you are at all worried, pour the gel down the side of a metal spoon or knife, which should absorb some of the heat and protect the container.

Though glass is the most obvious choice for a gel candle, you can also create some wonderful effects using shallow opaque containers, so that you look down on the candle. Try a tea bowl with a few real tea leaves suspended in pale golden-brown gel, a plain white bowl with one beautiful flower at the bottom, or a round bowl made of shiny metal which will produce an infinite number of reflections of the flickering candle flame. Whatever you decide to do, every gel candle will be unique.

pigments and dyes

You can buy ready-coloured gel to make candles, but I prefer to use clear gel and colour it myself. This can be done very easily, and I find it gives me a far greater range of possibilities.

One way to colour candles is with pure pigment (see right). This comes in large 50g (2oz) bags, so the initial outlay is fairly high. To begin with, you can buy just three primary colours (red, yellow and blue) and mix different shades. Once you have collected a range of different dyes and pigments, it will prove more economical.

The easiest way to work with pigment is to make up batches of gel, using strong concentrations of colour. Once set, these coloured gels will keep almost indefinitely in plastic containers. The batches of gel are easy to handle and you can make a wide range of colours. To use this intensely-pigmented gel, simply drop small pieces into clear gel as it melts.

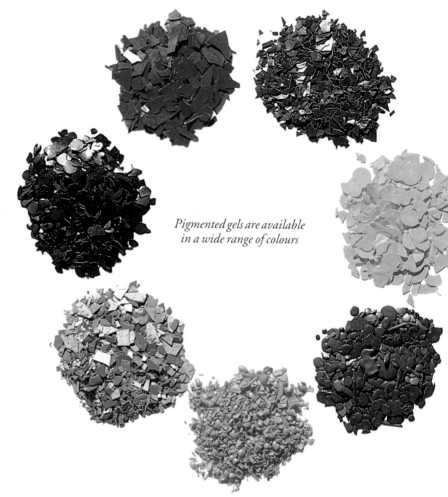

Pigmented gels are available in a wide range of colours

colouring your candle

If you need only a single shade of gel in your finished candle, it is fine to colour it with wax dye. Use the translucent variety, because solid wax dye makes gel go cloudy.

One of my most important discoveries, which the authors of many other books on the subject seem to have missed, is that you must use colouring matter appropriate to your finished candle. If you want to build up layers of different shades, and would like your candle to last a long time, you should mix your colours using pure pigment. Pigment produces stable colours, whereas dyes tend to bleed or migrate. If you make a striped candle using dye, the colours will eventually merge and the effect may be disappointing.

The photograph, left, shows two layered candles which were made with dyed gel and left for a few weeks. Though the effect at this stage is not unattractive, the candles will eventually become one-coloured.

pigmented gels

Pigmented gels are simple to make and, as the gel is oil-based, they will keep almost indefinitely without deterioration. The idea is to make a batch of gel with very strong pigmentation and allow it to set. You can make a wide range of colours and store them in sealed plastic containers to keep them clean and free from contamination. When you want to colour a candle, you simply break off a small piece of the pigmented gel and add it to clear gel. This saves time because you do not have to blend fresh pigments every time you want to make a small amount of coloured gel.

You will need
Hotplate
Saucepan
Thermometer
Clear gel
Pure pigment in desired colour
Baking tray (optional)

1. Melt 100g (4oz) of clear gel. Add 1g of powdered pigment. The more pigment you add, the more intense the colour will be.

2. Heat the saucepan of gel gently until the pigment dissolves, stirring it at intervals.

3. Pour the gel into a baking tray and let it set, or simply leave it in the pan. Lift it out carefully. Store in an airtight container.

perfumes

Gel candles lend themselves readily to the addition of perfumes, which will fill the room with a lovely aroma as the candle burns down. A wide range of different scents is available, making it possible to theme candles for extra interest. Why not try a pink-tinted candle with a strawberry perfume, or lemon gel with a fresh citrus tang added? The important thing to remember is to use and oil-based variety of perfume, as any other kind will simply evaporate. See page 12 for tips on how to test perfume for suitability.

Many different dyes and oil-based perfumes are available to scent or colour your candles. Add them with a dropper and take care not to use more than two per cent perfume.

things to embed

For a really attractive effect, you can incorporate a wide range of colourful and attractive items in your gel candles. This process is known as embedding. The most basic type of embedding, which is nevertheless extremely effective, is simply to stir some glitter into the molten gel. If you do this, make sure that the glitter is light enough not to sink to the bottom as the gel cools – the cosmetic type is ideal. You can also add perfume, but it must be oil-based and it is wise to test it first – see method below.

Another simple but effective way of embedding is to fix an item, for example a single dried flower (see page 32 for method) or a beautiful shell, to the bottom of the container and top it up with gel. As you gain confidence, you can begin to create dramatic effects or intricate themed scenes which will make your finished candles truly unique.

The third method of embedding is in layers, so that the items appear to be suspended in the gel. In this way, you can embed a wide range of items, but the process is slightly more complicated: each layer of gel must be allowed to cool before adding more items to prevent them from sinking to the bottom of the container. The good news is that almost anything is suitable for embedding, as nothing will rust in the oil-based gel. As long as you allow the layers to cool thoroughly, the gel will support quite heavy weights. A word of warning: if an item you wish to embed is porous, it is wise to seal its surface first to avoid bubbles in the candle. Shellac is usually ideal for this or soak in gel in a low oven until the bubbles stop rising.

It is important to remember not to place embedded items near the top of the container, unless, of course, your candle is intended to be purely ornamental. As the candle burns the area around the wick will liquefy, and items too close to the surface may migrate. This tip is especially important with flammable items such as dried flowers.

---

testing perfume

Perfumes must be oil-based: adding water-based substances to hot gel is dangerous. Candle perfumes are best but if you want to try out another kind, carry out the simple tests below:

1. The sniff test:
Dip a thin paper spill in the perfume, light it, then blow out the flame and sniff. This will tell you whether the perfume you have chosen has a pleasant aroma after burning.

2. The mixing test:
Melt a small amount of clear gel, add 2-3 drops of perfume, then pour into an egg-cup. Let it set, then remove it from the mould. Make sure the perfume has been incorporated with the gel: if it has separated out it will not be suitable for use in candles.

WARNING: your gel/perfume mix should not contain more than two per cent perfume or its combustion point might be affected.

Right: a selection of items suitable for embedding, including dried flowers, shells, glass nuggets, marbles, glitter, confetti, stone chips and beads. Use your imagination to create a unique candle.

equipment

saucepan

You can use any kind of saucepan for melting the gel, but I tend to use cheap enamel ones. I find that a white interior allows me to judge the finished shade of the gel, after adding any dye, pigment or pigment gel, more effectively.

hotplate

A plug-in electric hotplate with solid plates is easy to transport and clean. These come in single- and double-ring versions. If you use a domestic cooker, take care not to spill the gel on the rings.

thermometer

A thermometer is essential because it is important to check the temperature of the molten gel. I also find a thermometer useful for stirring the gel, though you can use a metal spoon or glass rod.

oven gloves

Have these handy at all times for holding hot pans and to move the candles while they are hot – the gel can give you a nasty burn if you are not careful.

wick needle

These long, thin needles are used across the top of your container to support the wick as the gel sets. An alternative is a fine meat skewer.

scales

These are useful for weighing ingredients. Cheap plastic scales are easy to clean, and can be kept just for use with gel candles.

paper towels

Have plenty of these handy for mopping up spills and wiping equipment – the gel can be messy.

wooden wedges

These are useful to support containers when pouring slanted layers. Cut prepared timber diagonally, or ask your local hardware store to help.

pliers

Use these to nip together the lugs on wick sustainers.

scalpel

You will find this useful for various tasks, including cutting card into strips for making moulds.

hairdryer

Use this to heat cold containers before use to minimise bubbling, or to 'blast' and re-melt gel which has set unevenly.

dropper

Use this to add drops of wax dye or perfume to your gel candle.

scissors

Use these to snip wicks to length.

tweezers

These are extremely useful for adjusting wicks in candles, fishing them out of paraffin wax, picking up small items for embedding etc.

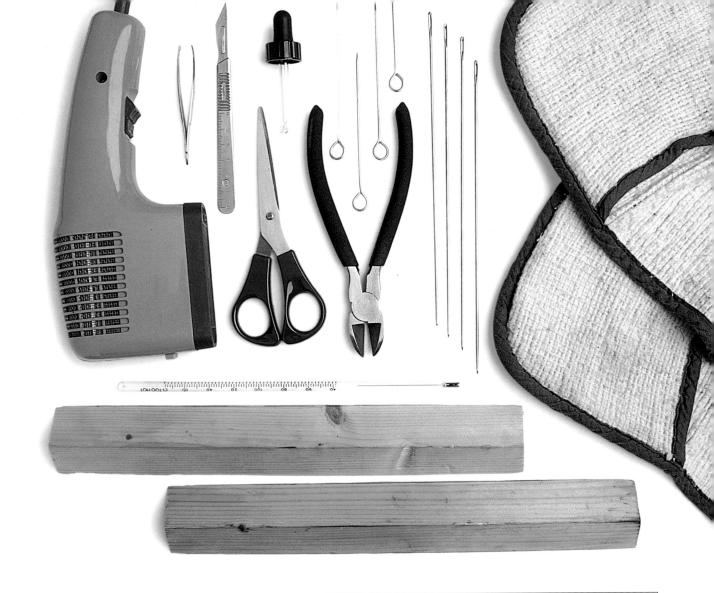

safety notes

- Do not ingest the gel. If it is swallowed, seek medical advice.

- Melt the gel in a pan over a low heat. DO NOT MICROWAVE.

- Remove the gel from the heat as soon as it becomes liquid.

- Do not leave the gel unattended while heating. Overheated gel will discolour and become highly inflammable.

- If you spill hot gel on your skin, immerse the affected area in cold water immediately.

- Glass and ceramics can sometimes shatter when heated. Choose your containers carefully.

- Perfume can increase the risk of the gel igniting. Make sure the proportion of perfume to gel does not exceed two per cent.

- Always place your candle on a flat, stable, heat-resistant surface.

- Protect woods, veneers and laminates with a heat-proof mat or a coaster.

- Do not burn a gel candle for more than four hours.

- NEVER leave a candle burning unattended.

- Do not burn candles near draughts, drapes or soft furnishings.

- Do not burn gel candles near embedded flammable materials, e.g. foliage, cardboard or plastics.

- Never burn the last half-inch of any gel candle.

In case of fire

- Turn off the power source to the hotplate.

- Smother flames with a pan lid or baking soda, or use a suitable fire extinguisher.

- Do not throw water on the flames, as it will make them spread.

Simple candles

You will need
Saucepan and hotplate
Thermometer
Glass container
Clear gel
Medium gauge wick and sustainer
Pliers
Wick needle
Scissors

The first project shows you how to make a simple candle with a fixed wick. You can also make gel candles with suspended wicks, but the basic method used for melting and pouring the gel is the same in every case.

To find out how much gel you will need, simply fill the container you have chosen, heaping the gel to allow a little extra. Put the gel in your pan, then wash your container thoroughly in hot soapy water to remove the oily gel residue. With a little practice, you will be able to estimate the amount of gel needed and cut out this measuring stage.

1. Put enough gel to fill your container into the pan and heat gently on a low setting until it melts.

2. Test the molten gel with the thermometer. For the best results, its temperature should be between 105°-110°C (221°-230°F)

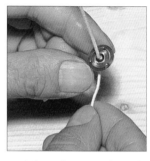

3. Thread a metal wick sustainer on to a length of wick.

4. Nip the sustainer with pliers to hold the wick firmly in place.

5. Measure the wick against the container and cut it to length, leaving a little extra to wind round the needle.

6. Trim the wick off under the sustainer, cutting in tightly.

7. Protect the work surface with paper. Position the wick and fix it in the container with gel.

8. Support the wick centrally in the glass by wrapping it round a wick needle.

The finished candle

9. Top up the candle with the rest of the gel. Leave it in a cool place until it has set firm.

10. Unwind the wick and trim it to length, leaving about 25mm (½ in) above the gel.

multiple wicks

If you want to use a large container – for example a wide, shallow bowl – you may want to use more than one wick. Some very attractive effects can be produced by putting more than one wick in a simple one-colour gel candle.

Try putting pretty pebbles on the bottom of a container, covering them with clear gel and using three or four wicks. Or make a candle using a stainless steel bowl, clear gel and several wicks. When you light the candle you will see how the flames seem to dance as they are reflected against the bright metal sides of the container.

17

suspended wick

For this candle, the wick is suspended in the gel instead of being fixed to the bottom. This technique is especially useful if you want to embed items, because there is no need to fix a wick sustainer to the bottom of the container. The candle wick is added to the completed candle when the gel has set firm. The only difference is that the wick needs to be treated first to make it stiff so that it can be inserted easily in the gel.

The following steps show you how to make pre-stiffened wicks using paraffin wax. It is a good idea to make a good supply and store them, then you will not have to make a fresh wick every time.

You will need
Two small saucepans
Clear gel
Liquid wax dye
Paraffin wax
Container
Medium gauge wick with metal core
Long wick needle or skewer
Tweezers
Thermometer

pre-stiffening the wick

1. Melt a handful of paraffin wax beads in a small saucepan or bain marie (double boiler).

2. Drop a length of wick in the molten wax. Leave until bubbles rise (about 30 seconds) and remove it with tweezers.

3. Let the wick cool slightly, then run it between your thumb and forefinger to straighten it. Set aside.

4. Heat the gel then, using a dropper, add a few drops of dye to colour it. Stir the gel thoroughly.

method

The finished candle

5. Protect your work surface with brown paper or newspaper. Pour the gel into the container. Let it set.

6. Heat the end of a long wick needle on the hotplate or in a gas flame. Insert it halfway into the candle to make a hole for the wick.

7. Working quickly, insert the stiffened wick into the hole made by the wick needle. Let it set, then trim the wick to the required length.

18

swirls of colour

A basic clear gel candle can be made far more interesting if you add a few swirls of colour. This is very easy to achieve using dried pigment, which comes in bags of what looks like small flakes of intense colour. Simply complete a basic candle, then drop flakes of one or more coloured pigments in the hot gel and stir to create the swirl effect.

The important thing to remember about making swirled candles is that you should not try to use wax dye. It is possible to create swirls using drops of dye, but they will not last! Wax dye is far less stable than pigment and the colours will soon migrate and merge so the swirls will disappear.

1. Complete a basic candle using clear gel and a fixed wick – see pages 16-17 steps 1-10.

You will need
Container
Wick
Wick needle
Clear gel
Pure pigment in two colours

2. Working quickly, drop in a few small flakes of pure pigment.

3. Swirl the gel with a thermometer or a glass rod until the effect you want is achieved.

4. Leave the candle undisturbed to cool. The pigment will move and change effect for some time.

5. Trim the wick to length to complete the candle.

tube-effect candle

An extraordinary effect can be achieved by putting a small container –
one of the thin metal tubes used for vitamin tablets is ideal – in your
gel as it sets. This creates a 'hole' in the gel, which can be filled up
with different colours made using a mixture of clear and pigmented
gel. For a really dramatic effect, pour stripes of different coloured gels
carefully down the hole. It is a bit fiddly, but well worth the effort.

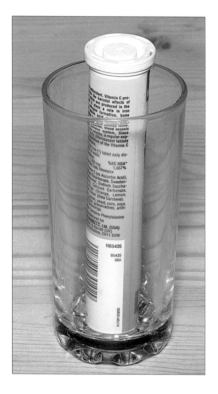

1. Place a small metal or plastic
tube in the container.

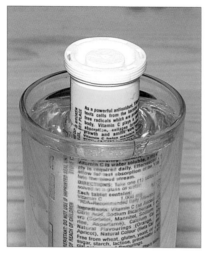

2. Fill the container with gel,
making sure that the tube stays
in the centre. Leave to cool.

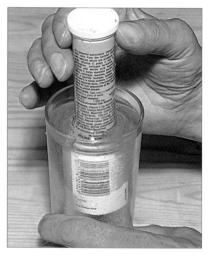

3. Remove the tube carefully
from the gel, using a slight
twisting motion to work it free.

4. Melt the rest of the clear gel
and add pigmented gel to colour
it. Pour the coloured gel carefully
into the 'hole' left by the tube.
Allow to set.

5. Heat a wick needle on the hotplate or in a gas flame. Insert in the
coloured middle section of candle. Remove, then insert stiffened wick.

Below: a trio of tube candles. The centre candle was made by pouring 'stripes' of gel in three different colours, alternating with clear gel, carefully down the hole left by the container.

Close-up of the tube candle

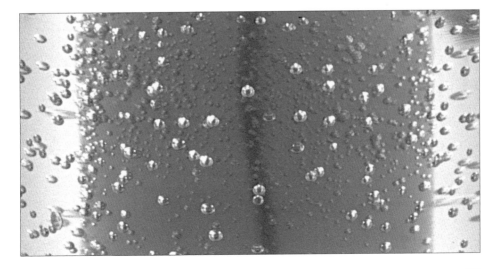

Layers & stripes

Pouring simple layers in different colours can result in some pretty spectacular effects for the minimum of effort. Each layer should be allowed to set before adding the next, and make sure the gel is not too hot or it may melt the previous layer. Remember that coloured layers should be made with pigmented gel (see page 11 for method). Do not use dye or the colours will soon merge.

(see page 11 for method)

<table>
<tr><td>You will need</td></tr>
</table>

You will need
Saucepan
Hotplate
Thermometer
Clear gel (enough to fill container)
Pigmented gel
Container
Wick and sustainer
Wick needle

simple layered candle

1. Wick up the glass and pour in a layer of clear gel to half way up the glass. Allow to set.

2. Heat half the remaining clear gel to between 105º-110ºC (221º-230ºF) and add a little ...mented gel to colour it. Pour :arefully on to the second layer gel and let it set.

Complete the candle by ...ling a third, clear layer, and ...n the wick to length.

Right: this variation shows the effect of layers of gel in rainbow colours

slanted layers

For this variation, the first and second layers have been poured while the glass container is held at a slant. I have done this by balancing the container between two wedges of wood – cut these yourself, or ask your local hardware store. The wedges can be secured to your work surface with pliable adhesive or modelling compound. Using the wedges ensures that each layer poured is at an accurate angle – in this case about 45 degrees. If you do not have wedges, you can improvise by propping the glass up using modelling compound.

You will need
Saucepan
Hotplate
Container
Clear gel
Pigmented gel
Wick and sustainer
Long wick needle
Wooden wedges
Pliable adhesive or modelling compound

1. Secure the wedges with pliable adhesive and use them to tilt the container. Heat some clear gel and pour into container.

2. Let the gel set, then stand the container up. Add red pigmented gel to the rest of the clear gel and use it to fill the container.

3. Leave the candle to set, then trim the wick to length.

This layered candle, right, shows how clear and pigmented gel set at different angles can produce interesting effects.

foam top

It is very easy to add a realistic 'foam' top to a finished candle by melting a small quantity of paraffin wax and whisking it as it cools, so that a thick consistency is obtained. The fluffy white foam looks particularly effective on a pale, golden-brown gel candle made in a tall glass – perhaps for your favourite lager drinker. It also works very well with a range of different 'cocktails' – remember the 'Snowball' grandma used to love?

You might also like to try using the foam to top a watery blue candle, perhaps containing a few sea creatures, some shells or even a model 'sunken' ship.

You will need
Lager glass
Clear gel
Orange and brown pigmented gel
Small saucepan
Hotplate
Thermometer
Wick and sustainer
Balloon whisk

2. Melt a little paraffin wax in a small pan

1. Make a basic candle, using clear gel with small amounts of orange and brown pigmented gel to produce a realistic 'lager' effect.

3. Remove from the heat and whisk the wax vigorously as it cools until it looks like foam.

4. Pour the 'foam' carefully onto the candle.

5. Use your finger to push the foam gently into place. Allow to set, then trim the wick.

The finished candle

27

Floating candles

It is extremely easy to make floating candles using gel: they can simply be stamped out using a metal or plastic pastry cutter. If you use wicks which have been stiffened first with paraffin wax, you can simply push them into the candle after removing it from the cutter. Take care not to make the candles too shallow or they may break when handled.

Opposite: a shallow bowl of floating hearts decorated with ivy makes a romantic table centrepiece.

You will need
Shallow glass container
Small saucepan
Hotplate
Thermometer
Clear gel
Pigment gel
Pastry cutter
Pre-stiffened wick

1. Melt some gel in a small saucepan. Add the desired colour pigment, then drop a small pastry cutter – plastic is fine – into the pan. The depth of the gel will be the depth of the finished candle.

2. Let the gel cool completely, then lift out the pastry cutter. The candle and the cutter will come out together.

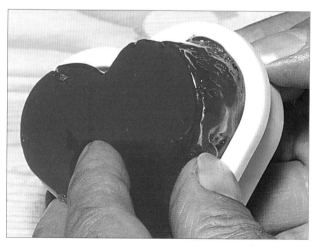

3. Remove the candle carefully from the mould. Make several candles, then push a short length of pre-stiffened wick in each and float them in a bowl.

Adding pzazz

A plain gel candle can be transformed into something special very simply by adding a few drops of perfume. Colouring the candle with a shade of dye or pigment which complements the perfume chosen will make it even more special. Another way to add interest very simply is by stirring a small amount of glitter into your candle before the gel cools. Do all three, and you can have a sparkly, prettily-coloured candle which gives off a delicious aroma as it burns. Make sure you test the perfume you have chosen for suitability before adding to the candle – see page 00 for tips and safety notes.

see page 00 for tips and safety notes.

You will need
Small saucepan
Hotplate
Saucepan
Thermometer
Dropper
Perfume
Clear gel
Pigment gel
Container
Wick needle
Wick and sustainer
Label (optional)

rose-perfumed candle

1. Melt clear gel, adding a little red pigment gel to colour it pink. Fix the wick in the glass with a little gel, and hold in place with a wick needle.

2. Test the temperature of the coloured gel and add perfume. You will need just a few drops.

3. Fill up the glass, working fast because the perfume evaporates if it is left in hot gel for too long.

4. Remove wick needle and trim wick to length. Add a pretty label if desired.

glitter candle

Make sure you buy cosmetic-grade glitter as other varieties may be too heavy and will simply sink to the bottom of the container. As glitter can be messy, protect your work surface with newspaper or brown paper which can be thrown away after use.

1. Wick up a container (see the method on pages 16-17). Melt some clear gel and add a small amount of cosmetic grade glitter.

2. Stir in the glitter thoroughly. Pour the glittery gel carefully into the container.

You will need
Saucepan
Hotplate
Thermometer
Container
Wick and sustainer
Wick needle
Clear gel
Cosmetic grade glitter
Teaspoon

Right: a selection of candles with glitter or perfume added

3. Let the gel set, then trim the wick to length.

Embedding

Almost anything can be embedded in a gel candle to make it more interesting, but flowers are among the most attractive items. Flowers must be dried before embedding to remove moisture, but it is easy to do this using silica gel – see the simple method below.

You will need
Fresh flower
Plastic container
Silica gel
Clear adhesive
Glass container

dried flower candles

1. Cover the bottom of a container with a layer of silica gel. Place a fresh flower in the silica gel and cover it completely.

2. Leave the container of silica gel to dry for a week, or put it in a microwave for twenty seconds. Pour off the gel carefully.

3. Put a dab of adhesive on the flower stalk, holding it carefully to avoid crushing the petals.

4. Glue the flower to the bottom of the glass and cover with clear gel. If you hear a slight fizzing, do not worry – it is just air trapped in the petals. Let the gel settle before pouring on the next layer. If there are still too many bubbles to see the flower clearly, put the container in a low oven (about 100ºC or 212ºF) for a few minutes to 'cook' them out.

right: the finished candle

opposite: a large stemmed bowl with embedded rose makes a delightful centrepiece for a table decoration

suspended objects

Some objects look better if they appear to 'float' in the gel rather than being fixed to the bottom of the container. The procedure for this is a little more complicated than simple embedding, as you will need to build up a layer of gel to support each layer of objects, allowing the layers to set before adding more gel. Surprisingly heavy objects can be embedded in this way. You must be sure to plan and pour your finished candle carefully: once it has set there is no going back, other than to prise out all the gel, melt it down and start again. You will not be able to put it into a hot oven to disperse bubbles, as doing so will simply melt all the layers and make all the embedded objects sink to the bottom!

key to the door

A key is a good simple first project for embedding in gel, and will also make an ideal novelty gift for a special birthday. You could use an ornamental key with the appropriate number on, but – as the gel will not harm metal or make it rust – why not use a real door key? Have a fresh one cut, as a shiny new key will look more attractive.

You will need
Saucepan
Thermometer
Hotplate
Clear and pigmented gels
Champagne glass
Key
Thin wire
Wick needle
Clear and pigmented gel
Pre-stiffened wick

1. Melt some clear gel and add pigmented gel to mix the right colour: tiny pieces of yellow and red should do the trick. Use wire and a wick needle to suspend a key in the glass.

2. Fill up the glass almost to the top of the key. Let the gel set, making sure it is really cool and firm.

3. Using scissors, snip the wire to free the key. Reheat the remaining gel and fill up the glass to the desired level.

Creating scenes

For me, one of the best things about using clear gel is that it can be used to create scenes which are actually in the candle. Unique candles can be created to celebrate a special occasion or to preserve and display a favourite memento. The technique resembles the acrylic embedding which was so popular a few years ago, with the advantage that gel does not damage the embedded item: it can be removed at any time.

Note: take care, when choosing items to embed, not to use endangered or protected species such as seahorses, coral or wild flowers.

You will need
Saucepan
Hotplate
Thermometer
Tall glass container
Strong adhesive
Wedding couple, doves and horseshoe
Long wick needle
Pre-stiffened wick

1. Choose a suitable container and fix a 'wedding couple' to the bottom with strong adhesive. Allow to set.

2. Plan your arrangement, using masking tape to mark the level where you want the doves to go.

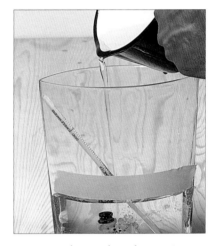

3. Heat clear gel and, pouring down the side of the thermometer to reduce any bubbling, fill the container to the level of the tape.

4. Position the doves carefully with tweezers, pushing them down into the gel slightly to embed them.

5. Pour on another layer of gel to cover the doves. Leave to set.

6. Position the horseshoe over the wedding couple, pushing it well into the gel to fix it firmly.

7. Fill the container to the required level with gel and allow it to set.

The finished candle
The wick was inserted by heating a long wick needle and pushing it into the gel, then pushing in a wick which was pre-stiffened by coating it with paraffin wax.

The candle viewed from directly above

grand piano

For the candle opposite, a tiny piano – in this case, a precious piece of dolls' house furniture borrowed from my daughter – was embedded in clear gel in a large, plain glass fish bowl. The final touches were added by a scattering of tiny gold foil musical notes above the piano, which catch the light and sparkle in the candle flame. Viewed from any angle, this candle is full of interest. It would make a perfect gift for a music lover, or a novel decoration for the buffet table at a musical evening or after-show party.

This close-up shows the gold foil musical notes

moon and stars

The celestial candle below would make an ideal gift for anyone interested in stargazing! The tall, elliptical vase allows the embedded foil moon and tiny stars to be seen easily from both sides. As this candle is made with only one colour, it does not matter whether you use pigment or dye to tint the gel blue.

The moon and star detail was made first, in the lid of a small container. The moon was set in a thin layer of clear gel, and arc was 'drawn' in the tacky gel using the points of scissors, to resemble the tail of a shooting star. A tiny star was placed at the top using tweezers.

The candle was made in the usual way, with a wick fixed to the bottom of the vase. A scattering of small stars was embedded in the gel using the layering technique shown on page 34. The gel disc was placed in the desired position against the side of the vase.

Note
If you want to make a similar candle, the gel disc does not need to be fixed in position with adhesive. It will cling quite happily to the side of the container while you pour the gel layers!

Moulded extras

As gel candles look particularly stunning made into multicoloured 'drinks', why not add the perfect finishing touch? Fruit slices are not only surprisingly easy to make, they are virtually indistinguishable from the real thing. The plaster moulds can be used over and over again – just store them in an airtight container and soak them in water to hydrate before use.

You will need
Lemon
Plaster of Paris
Cardboard ring
Small plastic bowl
Modelling material
Sieve
Plastic bowl

making moulds

1. Choose a firm fruit and cut a 6-12 mm (¼ - ½ in) slice.

2. Make a cardboard ring about 25mm (1in) larger all round than the slice of fruit.

3. Surround the ring with a long, narrow roll of modelling material to stop the plaster leaking out and keep it firm.

4. Put about 150ml (5fl.oz) of water in a plastic bowl. Sift in small amounts of plaster of Paris until all the water is absorbed.

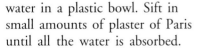

The mixed plaster should have an extremely thick consistency.

Note
Never wash your hands in the sink or pour unused plaster down the plug hole because it will solidify in the pipes and block the drains.

Rinse your hands in a bowl, then leave the water until the plaster solidifies in the bottom. Pick out the lumps and dispose of them by wrapping them in newspaper and placing them in the dustbin.

5. Working quickly before the plaster sets, pour it all over the slice of fruit. Leave it to set for about twenty minutes.

6. Melt a small quantity of clear gel and tint it lemon yellow using pigmented gel.

7. Remove the lemon slice, cardboard and moulding material from the mould. Damp it down, then pour in gel to coat it.

8. Quickly pour the gel back in the saucepan. The mould should be coated thinly with gel.

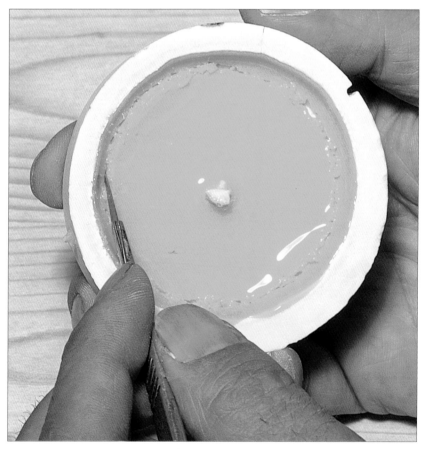

9. Using a scalpel, carefully incise a circle just inside the inner edge of the yellow gel.

10. Remove the circle of gel from the centre of the mould.

11. Melt some more gel and tint it white. Damp down the mould and pour in the white gel, then wait for it to set. Using a scalpel, incise a circle just inside the edge of the white gel. Remove the centre section, leaving a thin sliver of white gel round the edge.

12. Re-melt the remainder of the yellow gel and pour it into the mould. Leave the gel to set.

The finished lemon slice

13. Loosen the gel with a knife blade or scalpel and remove the finished lemon slice carefully.

gel cherry

Whole fruits are a little more fiddly to make, as the mould has to be made in two halves, but the effect can be terrific. The method detailed below is for a cherry, but is in fact suitable for any kind of spherical or roughly spherical fruit, from an olive to decorate a martini to a plum which can be 'bottled' in a preserving jar.

You will need
Plaster of Paris
Modelling wax
Modelling material
Rolling pin
Large pin or small nail
Cardboard
Teaspoon
Soap and brush
Screwdriver

1. Form the shape of a cherry using a piece of modelling wax.

2. Make a tiny solid cone from wax and secure it to the cherry shape with a pin or small nail.

3. Roll out some modelling material into a rough rectangle.

4. Using a teaspoon, scoop out a hemisphere from the modelling material to hold the wax cherry.

5. Scoop out a locating hole in each corner of the mould.

6. Surround the mould with cardboard and push in well.

7. Mix up some plaster of Paris (see page 41). Cover the cherry and funnel shape. Allow to set.

8. Remove the modelling material from the mould.

9. Leaving the moulded cherry in place, coat the mould with soap using a damp brush.

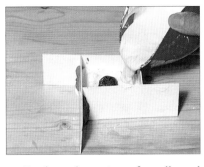

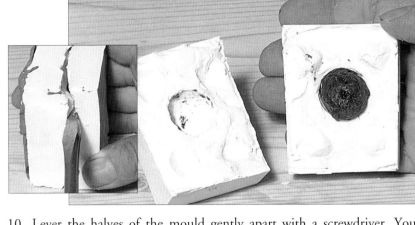

9. Replace the strips of cardboard and pour on more plaster to form the second half of the mould. The layer of soap will prevent the halves sticking together.

10. Lever the halves of the mould gently apart with a screwdriver. You will see a small hole left by the lug on the modelling wax cherry.

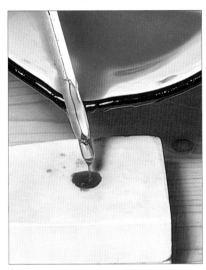

5. Remove the modelling wax cherry and soak the mould in water to hydrate it. Fit the two halves together with the hole uppermost. Heat some gel and colour it a realistic cherry red, then fill the mould with gel via the hole, pouring carefully down the side of a thermometer. Leave the gel to set, then carefully prise the mould apart.

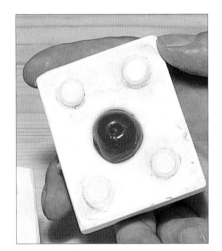

Right: the mould and the completed cherry

Jar of cherries
To make a really unusual candle, fill a preserving jar with gel fruit, cover it with clear gel which has been allowed to cool slightly, and add a wick

ringing the changes

Now you have mastered the techniques, you can make a wide range of fruits to add to your cocktails. Make orange slices using the same method as for lemon slices. Make a mould and pour in pale green gel for realistic olives. Bigger fruit like plums or apricots are effective in preserving jars.

Some ready-made moulds are also suitable, the most obvious of which is an ice-cube tray – the photograph below shows how effective gel ice cubes can be. Why not celebrate your new skills with a brightly-coloured gel cocktail topped with a gel cherry?

The lemon and orange slices and cherries were made in plaster moulds, while the realistic ice cubes were simply made using an ordinary ice cube tray.

Cocktail assortment
Gel fruit is the perfect complement to a dazzling array of bright cocktails that looks good enough to drink!

46

Index

A simple floating candle made from a rough lump of gel with a wick inserted